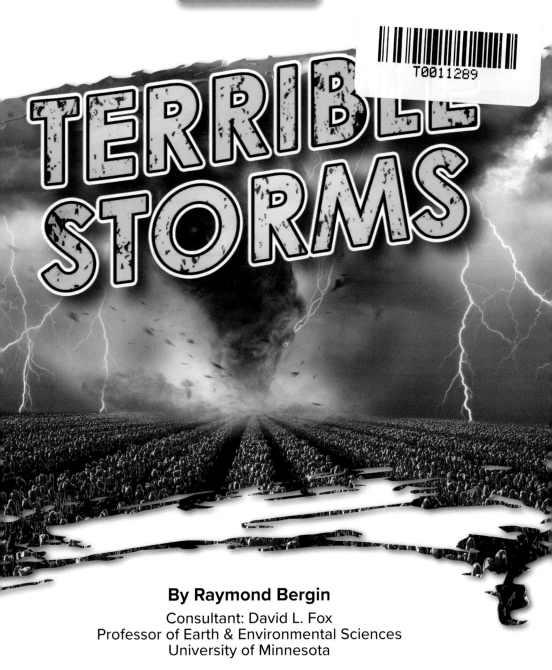

# TERRIBLE STORMS

## By Raymond Bergin

Consultant: David L. Fox
Professor of Earth & Environmental Sciences
University of Minnesota

**BEARPORT**
PUBLISHING

Minneapolis, Minnesota

## Credits

Cover and title page, © clintspencer/iStockphoto, © Oliver Henze/Alamy, © cosmin4000/iStockphoto, © D.Alimkin/Shutterstock; 4, © Michaelstockfoto/Shutterstock; 4–5, © john finney photography/Getty; 8–9, © Toa55/Shutterstock; 10, © thebigland/Shutterstock; 10–11, © underworld111/iStockphoto; 12–13, © piyaset/iStockphoto; 14–15, © mdesigner125/Getty; 16–17, © NPS Photo/Alamy; 18–19, © igorcorovic/iStockphoto; 19, © clintspencer/iStockphoto; 20, © DogoraSun/iStockphoto; 20–21, © NASA Johnson Space Center/Wikimedia; 22, © RoschetzkyIstockPhoto/iStockphoto; 23, © brazzo/iStockphoto; 25, © Janice and Nolan Braud /Alamy; 26, © Viktoriia Kovalova/iStockphoto; 26–27, © loveguli/iStockphoto; 28, © karamysh/Shutterstock; 29, © Jim Gimpel Photography/Shutterstock; , © Heymo/Shutterstock; , © Monkey Business Images/Shutterstock; , © P A/Shutterstock; , © Rawpixel.com/Shutterstock. **President:** Jen Jenson

**President:** Jen Jenson
**Director of Product Development:** Spencer Brinker
**Senior Editor:** Allison Juda
**Associate Editor:** Charly Haley
**Senior Designer:** Colin O'Dea

*Library of Congress Cataloging-in-Publication Data*

Names: Bergin, Raymond, 1968- author.
Title: Terrible storms / by Raymond Bergin.
Description: Minneapolis, Minnesota : Bearport Publishing Company, [2022] | Series: What on earth? climate change explained | Includes bibliographical references and index.
Identifiers: LCCN 2021034172 (print) | LCCN 2021034173 (ebook) | ISBN 9781636915593 (library binding) | ISBN 9781636915661 (paperback) | ISBN 9781636915739 (ebook)
Subjects: LCSH: Severe storms--Juvenile literature. | Climatic changes--Juvenile literature.
Classification: LCC QC941.3 .B48 2022 (print) | LCC QC941.3 (ebook) | DDC 551.55--dc23
LC record available at https://lccn.loc.gov/2021034172
LC ebook record available at https://lccn.loc.gov/2021034173

For more information, write to Bearport Publishing, 5357 Penn Avenue South, Minneapolis, MN 55419. Printed in the United States of America.

# Contents

# Weather Gone Wild

Winds whip along the coastline, blowing apart buildings and ripping up huge trees. Roads filled with water look more like rivers than streets. This huge hurricane should be the storm of the century. But violent hurricanes are becoming more common along the storm-battered coast.

Meanwhile, heat waves and **droughts** are drying out crop fields. Wildfires are tearing through **ancient** forests. And winter storms are knocking out power, which is sending whole communities into freezing darkness for days. What on Earth is causing these terrible storms?

The record-breaking 2020 Atlantic hurricane season included 30 **tropical storms** and 7 major hurricanes. It was the fifth straight year with an above-normal hurricane season.

# Planet Greenhouse

Earth is the only planet we know of with life—in part because it stays just the right temperature. During the day, sunlight warms Earth's land and water. At night, the day's heat rises up into the air. Gases in the air around Earth, known as **greenhouse gases**, make up a protective bubble and trap this heat. Like the inside of a greenhouse, the gases hold in the warmth needed for life. But this system that balances Earth's temperature is being thrown off by humans.

Not all of the sun's light stays on Earth. Some light is reflected off the bright surfaces of clouds, snow, and ice. This sends the light and heat back into space and keeps our planet from getting too hot.

**2** Some light bounces back into space.

**1** The sun's light comes to Earth. Its heat warms the planet.

**3** Some of the heat is trapped around the planet by greenhouse gases.

# More Gases, Warmer Earth

Greenhouse gases, such as **carbon dioxide**, are added to and removed from the **atmosphere** through natural processes. But everyday human activity also adds these gases. The **fossil fuels** oil, natural gas, and coal release lots of carbon dioxide when we burn them for power. As we drive our cars, heat our homes, and charge our devices, greenhouse gases are building up in the atmosphere. And they are trapping more and more heat.

Temperatures are rising and changing the **climate** worldwide. This creates unusual—and often wild—weather.

The years 2014–2020 were the planet's seven warmest years recorded to that point, and 2010 –2019 was the hottest decade.

# Heat Wave!

It's getting hot out there! Around the world, there are fewer cold days, and hot days are getting hotter. There are also more heat waves.

A heat wave is a streak of unusually hot weather that can last days or even weeks. The added greenhouse gases that are causing higher temperatures are also making heat waves hotter and longer. Fifty years ago, U.S. cities averaged only two heat waves a year. Now, they average six. And heat waves used to last an average of three days, but now that number is four.

Heat waves are more than just uncomfortable. They can also make you overheat and become ill. Heat sickness is one of the leading causes of weather-related deaths in the United States.

# Looking for Water

Because it's getting hotter, it's also getting drier in some places. Hotter weather dries out plants and soil. If there is little or no rain for a long time, the area goes into a drought. If a drought lasts a long time, crops and farm animals can die, which means less food for people. Fresh water sources for both animals and humans can also dry up.

There have always been droughts on this planet, but they're getting worse. Higher temperatures that come with global warming are making dry places even drier and making droughts last longer.

The American Southwest entered a megadrought in 2000. This dry spell has stretched on for more than two decades, becoming the region's worst drought since the 1500s.

# Dust in the Wind

As soil gets dried by drought, it becomes dusty. There is little or no **moisture** to keep it stuck to the ground. When strong winds blow through the very dry lands, they pick up the dust and carry it for hundreds of miles. These dust storms cause many problems. And they can even make global warming worse.

Sometimes, a storm can lift dust as high as 20,000 feet (6,100 m) into the air!

When this dust falls on **glaciers**, it makes their white surfaces darker. Then, the glaciers that would normally reflect the sun's heat **absorb** it. The heat warms the surrounding air and water even faster.

Scientists think dust storms will become more intense in the years ahead. A warming planet makes some places drier, which creates much more dust to be caught up and dropped by winds.

# Burning Out of Control

Like droughts, small wildfires are a natural part of forest life. They clear out dead leaves and plants to make more space for healthy new growth. But climate change has made larger wildfires more frequent—and far more damaging.

The warm, dry conditions are drying out more soil and plants. These dry lands burn hotter and more quickly when a fire starts. Stronger and faster wildfires are now damaging healthy plants as well. With little moisture in the land, wildfires quickly burn out of control.

Fire season is the time of year when wildfires are most likely to start and spread. With climate change, fire seasons worldwide have gotten longer—in some places as much as a whole month longer each year!

A wildfire from above

# Wet and Wild

While climate change is making some places drier, areas that do get rainfall are getting a lot wetter. Higher temperatures draw more moisture from the oceans, soil, and plants into the air. The warm, moist air rises and forms clouds. Eventually, the water falls down again as rain.

Since warmer air holds more water than cooler air, the rising temperatures in recent years have made rainfall heavier. In fact, 9 of the top 10 years for extreme rainstorms in the U.S. have been since 1996. These heavy **downpours** can ruin crops and cause dangerous and deadly flooding.

The same rising warm, moist air that creates rainfall can also form into tornadoes. Some scientists think the changing climate that is causing heavier downpours may also create more—and more powerful—twisters.

# Monster Storms

Warmer, wetter air is also helping create more hurricanes. These storms form when seawater rises into the air as tiny drops of water. Winds pull this air further upward. As the air rises, it cools and forms clouds. New air rushes in to replace the air that is rising, which creates a spinning motion. As more air rises, the spinning storm grows and winds increase speed. The warmer the air and the ocean, the more moisture and energy are drawn up into the hurricane— and the more serious the storm that may head toward land.

In 2017, Hurricane Harvey dumped almost 140 billion tons (127 billion t) of rain on Houston, Texas. In some places, more than 5 ft (1.5 m) of rain fell!

**A view of a hurricane from space**

# Storm Surge!

One of the greatest threats from a hurricane is when the storm pushes ocean water onto the shore. And this threat is made worse by climate change, too.

Most of the heat that is trapped by greenhouse gases is absorbed by the oceans. As a result, the oceans are getting warmer. When water is heated, it takes up more space, so **sea levels** rise and seawater washes farther up on shore. A hurricane's strong winds can push this high water even farther inland, creating a storm surge. This powerful rush of water can become a deadly and damaging flood.

In the United States, sea levels are rising fastest along the East and Gulf Coasts— exactly where hurricanes strike. Today, floods on these coasts happen five times more often than they did in the 1950s.

# Winter's Not Over!

Warmer temperatures are creating stronger droughts, rainstorms, and hurricanes. But sometimes even severe winter storms can be blamed on a planet that is heating up.

Strong winds usually keep very cold air locked up in the Arctic. But because of climate change, an unusual flow of warmer air can weaken the strong winds and cause the air to move. Sometimes, this **frigid** Arctic air travels as far down as the southern United States. So, places that don't usually get severe winter weather are now hit with heavy snowfall, freezing temperatures, or even extreme ice storms.

The warmer, wetter atmosphere can also create heavier snowstorms. Twice as many extreme snowstorms struck the United States in the second half of the 20th century, even though it was warmer than in the first.

Places in the south such as Texas (*pictured*) are not ready for the severed snow and ice storms that are hitting more frequently because of climate change.

# What Are We Doing about It?

People around the world are fighting climate change by reducing the amount of greenhouse gases they put into the atmosphere. Instead of burning fossil fuels, some people are using energy from the sun and wind to create electricity. Others are trying to protect the world and its people from the impacts of extreme weather. Still others are developing crops that grow during droughts and are planting **vegetation** along coastlines to help prevent flooding.

We're seeing stormy weather now, but the forecast will be much brighter if we all work together to fight climate change!

In many California towns and cities, thousands of goats are being put to work to **graze** the dry brush that can fuel wildfires. Each goat can eat 10 pounds (4.5 kg) of vegetation a day!

# Battle Terrible Storms!

How can you help fight climate change? Using less energy will help reduce the burning of fossil fuels. Cut down on how much you use electricity, heating, and gas to help battle terrible storms!

Electronics and chargers use power when they are plugged in—even if the device isn't in use. Unplug your chargers and electronics when you aren't using them.

When it's cold, keep the heat set low and wear warmer clothes. When it's hot, use a fan or keep your air conditioning at a higher temperature to use less energy.

Whenever it's safe and possible, walk or bike where you're going instead of taking a car.

To save water, take fewer and shorter showers. Don't keep water running when brushing your teeth or washing the dishes.

Join groups that clean up trash or replant trees near where you live.

# Glossary

**absorb** to take in or soak up

**ancient** very old

**atmosphere** a layer of gases that surrounds Earth

**carbon dioxide** a greenhouse gas given off when fossil fuels are burned

**climate** the typical weather in a place

**downpours** sudden heavy rains

**droughts** long periods of dry weather

**fossil fuels** fuels such as coal, oil, and gas made from the remains of plants and other organisms that died millions of years ago

**frigid** very cold

**glaciers** huge areas of ice and snow found on mountains and near the North and South poles

**graze** to eat grass or other vegetation

**greenhouse gases** carbon dioxide, methane, and other gases that trap warm air in the atmosphere so it cannot escape into space

**moisture** water contained in something, such as a cloud

**sea levels** the average height of the sea's surface

**tropical storms** circular storms that form over the ocean, with heavy rains and winds of between 39 and 73 miles per hour (63 and 117 kph)

**vegetation** different types of plants, including grasses, bushes, and trees

# Read More

**Blake, Kevin.** *Houston's Hurricane Harvey Floods (Code Red).* New York: Bearport Publishing, 2019.

**Dykstra, Mary.** *Climate Change and Extreme Storms (Searchlight Books. Climate Change).* Minneapolis: Lerner Publications, 2019.

**Finan, Catherine C.** *Weather (X-Treme Facts: Science).* Minneapolis: Bearport Publishing, 2021.

# Learn More Online

1. Go to **www.factsurfer.com** or scan the QR code below.

2. Enter "**Terrible Storms**" into the search box.

3. Click on the cover of this book to see a list of websites.

# Index

# About the Author

Raymond Bergin is a writer living in New Jersey, where he has experienced landfall of several Atlantic hurricanes. After Hurricane Sandy roared through the state in 2012, his home was without power for two weeks but, luckily, suffered no major damage.